How to Remember
EVERY CARD
in the Deck!

BOB HAMPTON

2 Time National Bridge Champion

ILLUSTRATED BY
Natalia Becerra

BARON BARCLAY
BRIDGE SUPPLY

How to Remember Every Card in the Deck!
Copyright © 2013, Bob Hampton

Baron Barclay Bridge Supply
3600 Chamberlain Lane, Suite 206
Louisville, KY 40241
U.S. and Canada: 1-800-274-2221
Worldwide: 502-426-0410
Fax: 502-426-2044

www.baronbarclay.com

ISBN 978-0-939460-49-6

Illustrations by Natalia Becerra
Cover design by Mary Maier
Text design and composition by John Reinhardt Book Design

Printed in Canada

Dedication

This book is dedicated to my two children, Mandi and Bobby, without whom my life would be incomplete. I wish to thank Steve Weinstein, Bobby Levin, Gavin Wolpert and all the top bridge professionals who took the time to teach me the intricacies of bridge. Joyce Hampton introduced me to duplicate bridge and gave me the opportunity to play with the best players in the world. For that, I am grateful.

Special thanks to Natalia Becerra, the talented artist whose illustrations in this book make my techniques come alive. I found her at the Art Institute in Henderson, Nevada. They have a spectacular program.

Contents

Introduction

HAVE YOU EVER WONDERED how many hearts are left or what happened to the Jack of Spades (you were sure it wasn't played yet!)? Have you ever lost count of one suit because you were focusing so hard on counting another suit? Have you ever lost a hand because the opponent just happened to have one more trump?

I think it's safe to say that all card players have had at least one of these scenarios happen to them probably more than once. It's not uncommon. It takes many top players years and years before they can count all the cards. For many others, it will never happen because remembering every card and in what order they were played is such a challenging task.

I am here to help. I will teach you how to remember every card in the deck and in what order they were played. I am an avid bridge player, and used my techniques to elevate my game. You can do the same, whether your game is Bridge, Canasta, Gin Rummy, Spades, Euchre, Poker, Blackjack or any other game where it helps to remember the cards. The process will take some effort on your part but it will be well worth it.

I would venture to guess that if average card players practice my techniques every day for sixty minutes, they will master memorizing cards within 14 days. Just think about it, if you can devote one hour a day for two weeks, you will rise to a level that you have never known before. It will be exhilarating to know how many cards of each suit have been played as well as the exact cards! You will have more knowledge of each person's hand. You will have more information to help you plan your game strategy. You will play your best after you learn to REMEMBER every card in the deck!

One
Get The Picture

I F I WERE TO TELL YOU that West played the ten of clubs, South already played the ace of hearts, North saved her five of diamonds till the end and East still has the three of clubs, you could probably remember that because right now you are really focusing. If I were to tell you that West had a bunch of CATS all over his head and shoulders, that South was wearing a huge HAT that almost touched the other players, that North was playing with a DOLL while playing her hand, and that East had a huge COMB that was bigger than his head stuck in his hair, you wouldn't forget it because the pictures are so vivid.

I first discovered duplicate bridge in 2003 on a world cruise. During my first year of tournaments I experienced some really hard lessons at the table. I kept thinking that there must be a way to become better, faster! The learning curve seemed so slow. Then, during the first half of my second year I realized that some people were making a concerted effort to memorize cards that had been played. There were other players who knew a lot of the cards that had been played but not all of the cards. I was the kind of player that people would love to play against because they would get great scores against me! The typical scenario would be that I would have two cards remaining and not remember which one to play. It was so frustrating!

Having taught memory classes all over Hawaii and California, I decided it was time to put those memory techniques to work! In August of 2005 I started developing my plan. It paid off when I won the Mini-McKenney that year as a sectional master (winning 790 points that year). Although I give most of the credit to the great players who were on my team, I still had to pull my own weight! My hard work paid off in August of 2009 when I won two national titles at the same national tournament in Washington D.C. I was part of the team that won the BAM (Board a Match) and also the Swiss teams. What a thrill!

I realized that there is a definite difference between remembering something (meaning how long can that item be remembered) and NOT FORGETTING something (meaning no matter what, you will not forget this item). This is the magic of "Memory", the ability to remember what is "IMPORTANT". Every card player has a certain capacity to remember cards. Some players are better at it than others. The top professionals are excellent at remembering every card because they have a gift for remembering the cards. Most of us are not born with that gift and have to develop another way to remember all the cards.

The irony is that when I talk with the very top bridge players like Bobby Levin or Steve Weinstein, they don't think they have a gift. They think everyone should be able to remember every card with practice. It's so easy for them that they just don't understand how hard it is for the rest of us. They will tell me that it takes years and years of playing and then it just happens. My reply is, "Oh really, what about players who have been playing decades longer than you and they still can't remember every card like you do?" They have no reply.

I wish I had their gift but I don't. However, I do have a gift for learning how to memorize. In fact, I would pit myself against any top bridge player in the world when it comes to memorizing cards. I would put up the challenge for someone to turn over a deck of cards, one card at a time, and then when the deck is done, pick any number from one to fifty-two and I will be able to recall instantly what card it is. I would be able to recall all 52 cards backwards, forwards, starting at a certain number, it doesn't matter. That's how reliable my memory techniques are. And now I'm going to teach them to you!

Two
Do You Remember?

The question now is, "Do you remember the cards that North, South, East and West had?" If you do, then you're one step ahead of the game. If you don't, do you remember what North was playing with? Do you remember what South had on her head that was almost touching other players? Do you remember what East had stuck in her hair? Do you remember what West was playing with while playing bridge? If you're like most people, then these pictures were much easier to recall than the cards themselves. Let's get started!

The first thing I need to teach you is that having a picture for a number is much easier than trying to picture a number. That might be a little confusing to some so let me restate that another way. Picturing a man playing with a DOLL is much easier to remember than trying to remember the Five of Diamonds being played from that man's hand. It is easier to have a picture that represents each card rather than trying to just remember numbers and suits. From now on, in fact, that DOLL will always represent the Five of Diamonds. Remember the CATS all over West? The CATS from now on will always represent the Ten of Clubs. What about the huge HAT that South wore? That HAT will always represent the Ace of Hearts. And what about East? Remember what East had in his hair? A huge COMB! From now on a COMB will always represent the Three of Clubs. Let me teach you how these words came to be.

Three
The Phonetic Alphabet

The phonetic alphabet takes letters from the alphabet and uses these letters to represent each number from 0-9. Only four consonants are not used to represent any number, they are:

Q, W, X, Y

Also, none of the vowels are used to represent any numbers. So, because vowels don't count for anything, we can use them to help make words that we can picture. Here's how it works.

These consonants will always represent these numbers:

0 = S or Z
1 = T or D
2 = N
3 = M
4 = R
5 = L
6 = SH, CH, soft G or J
7 = K, hard C or hard G
8 = F or V
9 = P or B

As you'll notice, some numbers have more than one consonant sound. This is not a problem because you will only have to use one sound to represent each number. You even get to pick which sound you want to use for the numbers that have more than one consonant sound. For example, you could decide to use the T instead of the D sound for number one. Either one works because they both represent number one. The reason there is more than one sound for some of the numbers is because if you were to pronounce these sounds (such as the T or D sound for number 1), then you'd notice that your mouth moves exactly the same way. Although the SH, CH, soft G or J are four different choices for number 6, your mouth moves exactly the same way. For example, CACHE and CASH are spelled differently but are pronounced exactly the same. Therefore, both of these words would represent the number 76 (Hard C for the 7 and the SH sound for the 6).

Remember that vowels count for nothing and are simply used to connect the consonants together to form words. Also, remember that this is a phonetic alphabet, so that means we only count SOUNDS. For example, the word COMB would only represent 73 (Hard C for the 7 and the M sound for the 3). Even though the B is at the end of the word, it is silent and therefore not counted.

Let's practice a little. First, I will give you a few examples and then I will give you a quiz. The word FARM would represent the number 843 (F=8, R=4, M=3). The word CHOSEN represents the number 602 (CH=6, S=0, N=2).

The word CHERRY represents the number 64 (CH=6, R=4, remember that you only hear one R sound and the other is silent). Your turn!

Chapter 3 Quiz

What number do these words represent?

1. COT
2. DOT
3. AT
4. SHOT
5. COFFEE
6. DOVE
7. GIVE
8. CAFÉ
9. CASH
10. DISH
11. ITCH (Tricky, careful)
12. TACK
13. COOKS
14. DUCKS
15. LOOKS
16. TRUNKS

How Did You Do?

ANSWERS:

1. 71
2. 11
3. 1
4. 61
5. 78 (Only one F sound is heard, the other is silent)
6. 18
7. 78
8. 78
9. 76
10. 16
11. 6 (The only sound heard is the CH sound)
12. 17
13. 770
14. 170
15. 570
16. 14270

Four
The Phonetic Alphabet and Cards

Now that you have learned the basics of the phonetic alphabet, let's use this alphabet to memorize cards! Every card has a face value from the ACE through the KING. The Ace through the Ten will have their normal value as follows:

ACE = T or D

   2 = N

   3 = M

   4 = R

   5 = L

   6 = SH, CH, soft G or J

   7 = K, hard C or hard G

   8 = F or V

   9 = P or B

 10 = T or D (representing the 1) plus the S or Z (representing the 0)

I will talk about the face cards in a moment. Now that we have all the numbers down from Ace through Ten, let's get started on the suits. We'll start with the lowest suit or Clubs. We will place the letter C (representing the Club suit) at the start of each word and then use our phonetic alphabet after the first letter to represent the number of that suit. For example, let's take the 4 of Clubs. The C will be the first letter of the word because the card is a Club. Now we will put an R next to the C because the R represents number 4. Next we'll take our vowels, which count for nothing, to put between the C and the R and make the word CAR. So, from now on, when someone at your table plays the 4 of Clubs, picture a huge CAR on top of her head. Make it a ridiculous picture like the car is revving its engine really loudly or squishing her neck down. The more ridiculous the picture the more you will remember which player had that card. Let's continue with the rest of the Club suit.

Clubs

ACE of CLUBS = CoT (C for Clubs and T for 1 or Ace)

TWO OF CLUBS = CaN (C for Clubs and N for 2)

THREE OF CLUBS = CoMb (C for Clubs and M for 3. Remember the b is silent and not counted)

FOUR OF CLUBS = CaR (C for Clubs and R for 4)

FIVE OF CLUBS = CeLL (C for Clubs and L for 5. Remember you only hear one L)

SIX OF CLUBS = CaSH (C for Clubs and SH for 6)

SEVEN OF CLUBS = CoKe (C for Clubs and K for 7)

EIGHT OF CLUBS = CoFFee (C for Clubs and F for 8. Remember only one F is heard)

NINE OF CLUBS = CoP (C for Clubs and P for 9)

TEN OF CLUBS = CaTS (C for Clubs and TS for 10)

Here's What Your Pictures Might Look Like for Clubs...

Now Let's Do Diamonds

ACE of DIAMONDS   =   DoT (D for Diamonds and T for 1)

TWO of DIAMONDS   =   DaNe (This is like a great DaNe dog. D for Diamonds and N for 2)

THREE of DIAMONDS =   DaM (D for Diamonds and M for 3)

FOUR of DIAMONDS   =   DooR (D for Diamonds and R for 4)

FIVE of DIAMONDS   =   DoLL (D for Diamonds and L for 5. Remember only one L is heard)

SIX of DIAMONDS   =   DiSH (D for Diamonds and SH for 6)

SEVEN of DIAMONDS =   DoC (D for Diamonds and C for 7)

EIGHT of DIAMONDS   =   DoVe (D for Diamonds and V for 8)

NINE of DIAMONDS   =   DiP (D for Diamonds and P for 9)

TEN of DIAMONDS   =   DaTeS (D for Diamonds and TS for 10)

Here's What Your Pictures Might Look Like for Diamonds...

Now Let's Do Hearts

ACE of HEARTS　　　= HaT (H for Hearts and T for 1)

TWO of HEARTS　　 = HeN (H for Hearts and N for 2)

THREE of HEARTS = HaM (H for Hearts and M for 3)

FOUR of HEARTS　 = HaiR (H for Hearts and R for 4)

FIVE of HEARTS　　= HaiL (H for Hearts and L for 5)

SIX of HEARTS　　　= HitCH (H for Hearts and CH for 6. Remember the t is silent)

SEVEN of HEARTS = HawK (H for Hearts and K for 7)

EIGHT of HEARTS = HiVe (H for Hearts and V for 8)

NINE of HEARTS　 = HooP (H for Hearts and P for 9)

TEN of HEARTS　　 = HuTS (H for Hearts and TS for 10)

Here's What Your Pictures Might Look Like for Hearts...

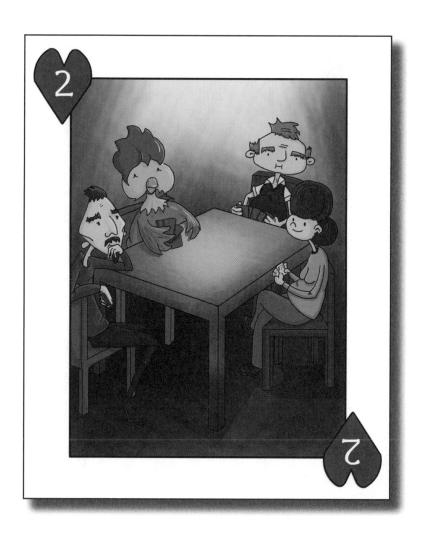

Now Let's Do Spades

ACE of SPADES = SoT (S for Spades and T for 1)

TWO of SPADES = SuN (S for Spades and N for 2)

THREE of SPADES = SaM (S for Spades and M for 3)

FOUR of SPADES = SoRe (S for Spades and R for 4)

FIVE of SPADES = SaiL (S for Spades and L for 5)

SIX of SPADES = SaSH (S for Spades and SH for 6)

SEVEN of SPADES = SocK (S for Spades and K for 7. The c is silent so you don't count it.)

EIGHT of SPADES = SaFe (S for Spades and F for 8)

NINE of SPADES = SaP (S for Spades and P for 9)

TEN of SPADES = SeaTS (S for Spades and TS for 10)

Here's What Your Pictures Might Look Like
for Spades...

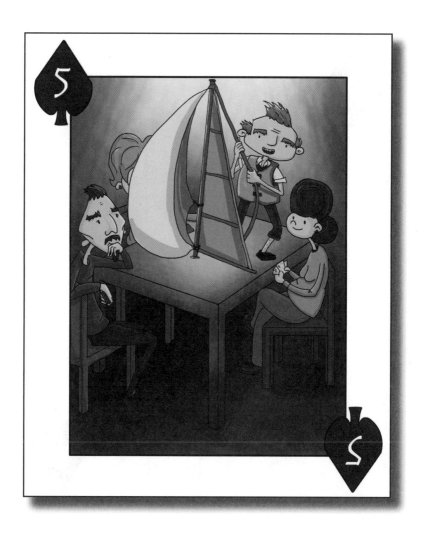

Here's The Entire List So Far
From Ace Through Ten

Card #	Clubs	Diamonds	Hearts	Spades
Ace	COT	DOT	HAT	SOT
2	CAN	DANE	HEN	SUN
3	COMB	DAM	HAM	SAM
4	CAR	DOOR	HAIR	SORE
5	CELL	DOLL	HAIL	SAIL
6	CASH	DISH	HITCH	SASH
7	COKE	DOC	HAWK	SOCK
8	COFFEE	DOVE	HIVE	SAFE
9	COP	DIP	HOOP	SAP
10	CATS	DATES	HUTS	SEATS

One of the great things about the phonetic alphabet is that on some numbers I have a selection of different consonants I can choose from. For example, on the number 8 I can use the F or the V. As you can see it was easier to use the F for Clubs and Spades and the V for Diamonds and Hearts. Either choice is fine because I know that F or V is always representing 8.

Five
Let's Practice

BEFORE WE GET to the face cards, let's practice and make sure you have Ace through Ten down. See if you can remember the pictures that represent these cards:

1. Ace of clubs
2. Four of clubs
3. Three of hearts
4. Six of hearts
5. Seven of spades
6. Nine of spades
7. Two of diamonds
8. Eight of diamonds
9. Ten of diamonds
10. Four of spades
11. Nine of hearts
12. Ten of clubs
13. Ace of hearts
14. Five of clubs
15. Five of spades

Answers To Let's Practice

1. CoT
2. CaR
3. HaM
4. HitCH
5. SocK
6. SaP
7. DaNe
8. DoVe
9. DaTeS
10. SoRe
11. HooP
12. CaTS
13. HaT
14. CeLL
15. SaiL

In order to effectively remember these pictures, it is imperative that you make the silliest picture as possible. For example, on number 14 the card is the five of clubs. When someone plays this card, picture long metal bars that automatically drop down around her. See her expression. Hear the thud as the bars drop! The person is now enclosed in a cell as if she were in prison! The more ridiculous detail you can put into your picture the more likely you are to remember it.

Six
What About Face Cards?

U P TO THIS POINT you have learned how to memorize 40 cards, the ace through ten. Now it's time to teach you how to memorize the face cards.

You will recall that every card from ace through ten has the first letter (a consonant), which represents the suit, and the last letter (a consonant), which represents the number of the card. You have also learned that you only count the sounds that are heard. So, for a single digit number you should only hear two consonants, the first representing the suit and the second representing the number. A good example would be the 5 of spades or "SaiL". The "S" represents the suit, spades, and the "L" represents the 5 from the phonetic alphabet. Another single digit is the 5 of diamonds or "DoLL". The D represents the suit, diamonds, and the L represents the 5 from the phonetic alphabet. Remember that you only hear one L sound so only one is counted.

Our next step is memorizing the face cards. This is how we are going to do it. A single word will represent each face card. The first letter of the word (a consonant) will represent the suit, and the second consonant sound will represent the face card. This is a little different from the number cards because no matter how many consonant sounds we hear, ONLY the second consonant sound will represent the face card. Take, for example, the queen of spades. The word "Squirrel" could be formed with the first consonant or "S" representing the spade suit and the second consonant or "Q" representing the Queen. Any letter after the second consonant sound is irrelevant and counts for nothing.

Here's what the list looks like:

Clubs

JACK of CLUBS	=	CaJun (C represents clubs and J represents the Jack)
QUEEN of CLUBS	=	CoQuette (C represents clubs and Q represents the Queen)
KING of CLUBS	=	CooKs (C represents clubs and K represents the King)

Diamonds

JACK of DIAMONDS	=	DJ (D represents diamonds and J represents the Jack)
QUEEN of DIAMONDS	=	DaQuiri (D represents diamonds and Q represents the Queen)
KING of DIAMONDS	=	DucKs (D represents diamonds and the K sound represents the King)-remember it is only the sound that is counted. You never hear the "c" in DucKs, only the "K" sound.

Hearts

JACK of HEARTS = HeJaa! (Pronounced like a karate chop. H represents hearts and J represents the Jack.)

QUEEN of HEARTS = H.Q. (H represents hearts and Q represents the Queen.) For this one I like to think of Head Quarter. When someone plays that card, I will picture her head as a huge quarter.

KING of HEARTS = HooKs (H represents hearts and K represents the King)

Spades

JACK of SPADES = SaGe (S represents spades and the J sound represents the Jack)

QUEEN of SPADES = SQuirrel (S represents spades and the Q represents the Queen)

KING of SPADES = SKunk (S represents spades and the K represents the King)

Here's What Your Face Card Pictures Might Look Like
for Clubs...

Here's What Your Face Card Pictures Might Look Like for Diamonds...

Here's What Your Face Card Pictures Might Look Like
for Hearts...

Here's What Your Face Card Pictures Might Look Like for Spades...

Here's our final face card list:

Clubs	Diamonds	Hearts	Spades
Jack = CaJun	Jack = D.J.	Jack = HeJaa!	Jack = SaGe
Queen = CoQuette	Queen = DaQuiri	Queen = H.Q.	Queen = SQuirrel
King = CooKs	King = DucKs	King = HooKs	King = SKunk

Seven
Let's Play Cards!

YOU HAVE NOW LEARNED how to memorize every card in the deck. A word of advice is to give yourself plenty of time before practicing these techniques at a tournament! A good estimate would be to give yourself two weeks, practicing at least one hour every day, before using these techniques in competition. It may be more or less time for some.

There will be many hands that will not require the use of any memory techniques. There will be many other hands that will require memory techniques for only one or two suits. And, there will be many other hands that will require memory techniques for every card! Whatever card game you play and whether you play cards competitively or socially, if you have mastered these techniques you will have a great advantage.

Good luck, and REMEMBER to have fun!

The Final List

Card #	Clubs	Diamonds	Hearts	Spades
ACE	COT	DOT	HAT	SOT
2	CAN	DANE	HEN	SUN
3	COMB	DAM	HAM	SAM
4	CAR	DOOR	HAIR	SORE
5	CELL	DOLL	HAIL	SAIL
6	CASH	DISH	HATCH	SASH
7	COKE	DOC	HAWK	SOCK
8	COFFEE	DOVE	HIVE	SAFE
9	COP	DIP	HOOP	SAP
10	CATS	DATES	HUTS	SEATS
Jack	CAJUN	D.J.	HEJAA!	SAGE
Queen	COQUETTE	DAQUIRI	H.Q.	SQUIRREL
King	COOKS	DUCKS	HOOKS	SKUNK

About The Author

BOB HAMPTON, of Henderson, NV, is one of the country's most successful memory teachers. Since 1986, he has taught classes and individuals across the U.S. and helped everyone from school children to business men and women to actors. Bob started learning memory techniques because of poor grades due to attention deficit disorder. After applying memory techniques, his grades soared from a 2.3 in undergraduate studies to a 3.7 in his masters degree at Brigham Young University. In 2005, he developed a plan to put memory techniques to work remembering cards, and went on to become a national bridge champion in 2009.

About The Illustrator

NATALIA BECERRA, of Henderson, Nevada, graduated from the Media Arts & Animation program at The Art Institute. She is constantly looking for new things to learn, creative ideas to share and different ways to express those ideas. Her passion for art has led her to explore the diverse possibilities offered by animation, illustration and sculpting.